BOWLING

Don Cruickshank

WEIGL PUBLISHERS INC.

Published by Weigl Publishers Inc.
350 5th Avenue, Suite 3304, PMB 6G
New York, NY 10118-0069

Copyright © 2007 Weigl Publishers Inc.
www.weigl.com

Library of Congress Cataloging-in-Publication Data

Cruikshank, Don.
   For the love of bowling / Don Cruikshank.
    p. cm. — (For the love of sports)
   Includes index.
   ISBN 1-59036-384-1 (hard cover : alk. paper) — ISBN 1-59036-385-X
(soft cover : alk. paper)
1. Bowling—Juvenile literature. I. Title. II. Series.
GV902.5.C78 2006   794.6—dc22   2005026965

Printed in the United States of America

1 2 3 4 5 6 7 8 9 10 09 08 07 06

Editor
Frances Purslow

Cover and page design
Terry Paulhus

Cover: Each bowling pin needs to tilt only 7.5 degrees in order to fall down, but flying pins often knock down others.

Photograph Credits
PBA LLC: Page 11; **United States Bowling Congress:** Pages 16R, 17L, 17R, 18L, 19L; **PB3 Entertainment:** Page 19R (Leslie Bohn).

Contents

All about Bowling

Bowling is a game played in more than 120 countries. It is a popular sport. More than 100 million people bowl each year. In the United States, more than 3 million bowlers bowl in tournaments.

Bowling is an **individual sport**. However, bowlers often play on teams in leagues. They play in a bowling center or bowling alley. Bowling centers are divided into sections called lanes. A lane is a runway with 10 pins set up at the far end. Players try to knock the pins down by rolling a bowling ball down the lane. The goal of the game is to knock down all 10 pins.

Pin boys set up bowling pins by hand in 1909.

Nine-pin bowling was outlawed in the 1840s because of gambling. Many people believe 10-pin was invented so that people could continue bowling.

Bowling is a game with a long history. In the 1930s, a famous British **Egyptologist** named Sir Flinders Petrie entered a tomb and found objects that may have been used to play a form of bowling thousands of years ago. The first public bowling center was established in London, England, in the fifteenth century. The first bowling tournament was held in Germany in the city of Breslau in 1518. First prize was an ox!

Bowling was played in Europe long before it came to North America. At that time, there were nine pins. Then, in 1870, another pin was added, and 10-pin bowling was invented. New York is the birthplace of 10-pin bowling. In 1895, the rules of bowling were set by the American Bowling Congress.

CHECK IT OUT

Read more about bowling's history at **www.bowlingmuseum.com**

Getting Started

Bowlers need very little special equipment to play the game. Most players wear casual pants and shirts that allow them to twist and turn easily when rolling the ball.

Rosin is used to help grip the ball.

Wrist supports are worn by some bowlers to prevent their wrists from bending.

Equipment bags contain a player's ball, shoes, and towel. Players may use a towel to wipe oil or dirt off the ball.

Early bowling balls were made of rubber. Today, most balls are made of plastic. Bowling balls are between 8 and 16 pounds (3.6 to 7.2 kilograms). They are about 8.5 inches (21.5 centimeters) in diameter.

Plastic balls are faster and easier to hook than rubber balls. Experienced players can hook the ball to the left or right. They do this to increase their chances of improving their score.

Stronger players may prefer a heavier ball. Smaller players with less strength may prefer a lighter ball. Heavy balls knock down more pins than light balls. Still, players need to choose a ball they can control.

Bowlers wear special bowling shoes. The shoes have a leather sole on one foot for sliding and a rubber tip on the other for gripping.

The Bowling Center

When players arrive at a bowling center, they are assigned a bowling lane. There is a scoring table and seating area behind each lane. This is where bowlers put on their shoes and await their turn to bowl.

Each lane consists of the **approach**, the lane itself, and the pin area, or deck. A foul line separates the approach and the lane. A player steps onto the approach and picks up the ball from the ball rack. Then he or she takes about four steps to the foul line and throws the ball down the lane. There are spots and arrows on the approach and the lane. They help players aim the ball.

Most modern bowling alleys have computerized scoring that appears on a TV hanging above the lane.

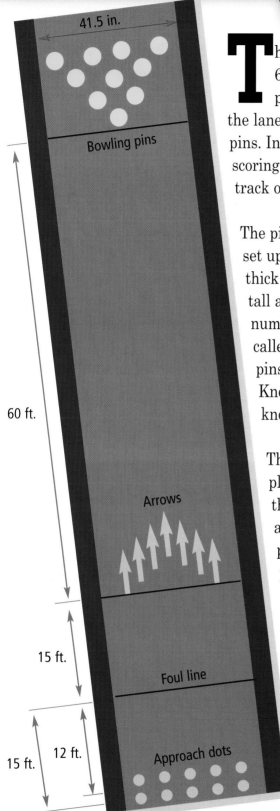

41.5 in.

Bowling pins

60 ft.

Arrows

15 ft.

Foul line

15 ft.

12 ft.

Approach dots

The lanes are 41.5 inches (1.1 meters) wide and 60 feet (18 m) long. They are made of maple and pine boards. There is a **gutter** on either side of the lane. Balls that land in the gutter roll and miss the pins. In some bowling centers, there is an automatic scoring machine above the lane. This machine keeps track of the score.

The pin area, or deck, is where the 10 bowling pins are set up. The pins are made of wood and covered with a thick plastic coating. Each pin is 15 inches (38 cm) tall and weighs about 3.5 pounds (1.64 kg). They are numbered from one to ten. The number one pin is called the headpin because it is in front of the other pins. The number five pin is called the kingpin. Knocking it over increases a player's chance of knocking all of the pins down.

There is a pin indicator above the deck. It shows players which pins are left standing after a ball is thrown. The pins that are knocked down bounce against cushions and land in a pit. After a player's turn is complete, the **automatic pinsetter** picks up the pins that fall and sets them up for the next bowler. The pinsetter also sends the ball back to the approach through an underground **ball return**.

CHECK IT OUT

Try some virtual bowling games at **www.bowl.com** *Click on Games.*

Rules of the Game

A bowling game consists of 10 frames. Players are allowed to deliver up to two balls in each frame. The goal in each frame is to knock down all 10 pins. Players who knock down all 10 pins in the tenth frame are allowed a third ball. The third ball is called a bonus ball.

Players bowl in order. Each player bowls one frame at a time. The game is over when every player has completed 10 frames. Between two to six people usually play in a game.

Players must deliver the ball from the approach. If the player's foot crosses the foul line during the delivery of the ball, no points are awarded for that ball. There are also no points awarded for a ball that ends up in the gutter.

	Frames													Score
Kelly	4 5 / 9	2 ◢ / 20	1 2 / 23											
Parker	■ / 18	7 1 / 26												
Mike	– 2 / 2	9 / 11												

■ **Strike**   ◢ **Spare**

The highest score in bowling is 300.

Every player has an average. A bowler's game scores are added up. Then that total is divided by the number of games that player has played. The answer is the player's average. Professional bowlers have averages in the low 200s. **Amateur** bowlers must maintain an average of 200 for two years to qualify for the Professional Bowlers Association (PBA) tour.

Parker Bohn holds the best annual average in PBA history. It is 228.04.

CHECK IT OUT

Make your own bowling puzzle at http://puzzlemaker.school.discovery.com Select "Word Search" from the Try other puzzles! field.

Bowling Shots

Players use special words to describe their scores. Knocking down all 10 pins in a frame with the first ball is called a strike. Knocking down all 10 pins in a frame with two balls is called a spare. An open frame occurs when there are pins left standing after the second ball.

Bowlers roll four types of shots, or balls. They are the hook ball, the curve ball, the straight ball, and the backup ball. The hook ball is the best for making strikes. It hits the headpin and the number one pin at the angle most likely to knock down all of the pins. The curve ball is not as effective as the hook ball for two reasons. First, the curve ball moves more slowly and with less force than the hook ball. Second, the curve ball is harder to control because it makes a bigger curve than the hook ball. The straight ball hits the pins straight on and does not produce many strikes. It usually hits the number three pin with too much force and the kingpin with too little force. The backup ball is seldom used. It is not a very fast or powerful ball. Players have to twist their wrists in an awkward way to throw a backup ball.

A straight ball will often knock down the middle pins, leaving the side pins standing. This is know as a split.

Beginners often think a heavy ball and a hard throw will make more strikes and spares. This is not always true. To make strikes and spares, players need to use control and technique, not strength. Control and technique come with practice.

Bowling is a popular activity with families because all ages can play together.

CHECK IT OUT

Read more about bowling at
http://encarta.msn.com

Type Bowling into the Search field.

Where the Action Is

The PBA **governs** professional men's bowling in the United States. The Professional Women's Bowling Association (PWBA) governs professional women's bowling. Male professional bowlers play on the PBA tour. Women take part in the PWBA tour. These tours consist of bowling tournaments. Most professional bowlers have other jobs. Some work as instructors or bowling center operators. Others have jobs outside the bowling industry.

Walter Ray Williams won Best Bowler at the 2003 Excellence in Sports Performance Yearly Awards. He has also won dozens of PBA titles.

There are thousands of bowling tournaments every year. The most important professional men's tournaments are the PBA National, The Tournament of Champions, the U.S. Open, and the ABC Masters. The grand slam of bowling is awarded to players who win all four of these tournaments. The triple crown of bowling is awarded to players who win the PBA National, the Tournament of Champions, and the U.S. Open.

The most important amateur tournament is the AMF Bowling World Cup. The AMF is hosted by a different country every year. In 2004, Shannon Pluhowsky from the United States was one of the champions in Singapore. That year, more than 90 countries competed in the AMF World Cup.

Bowling tournaments are a popular way to raise money for charities. Bowling for Backpacks raised money for Hurricane Katrina survivors.

The most important professional women's tournaments are the U.S. Open, the WIBC Queens, and the Sam's Town Invitational. These tournaments are the women's triple crown of bowling. The most important amateur tournament for women is the AMF World Cup.

Pioneers of the Sport

Bowling has provided many hours of entertainment for people who play the sport or watch it on television.

DON CARTER

Career Facts:

- Bowling fans and those who knew Don referred to him as "Mr. Bowling" because of his passion for the sport.
- He also won the All-Star tournament in 1952, 1954, 1956, and 1958.
- Don was named PBA Bowler of the Year in 1953, 1954, 1957, 1958, 1960, and 1962.
- Don was inducted into the PBA Hall of Fame in St. Louis, Missouri, in 1975.
- Don Carter served as PBA president for two years.

DICK WEBER

Career Facts:

- Dick won PBA Bowler of the Year in 1961, 1963, and 1965.
- Over five decades, Dick won four All-Star titles, 11 All-American Team honors, 24 PBA tournaments, and 6 senior titles.
- Dick was inducted into the PBA Hall of Fame in 1975. His son, Pete, joined him in the Hall of Fame in 1998.

LOUISE FULTON

Career Facts:

- In 1964, Louise became the first African American woman to win a professional bowling title.

- She first bowled in a **rubberband duckpin** league. Then she moved on to 10-pin.

- She had a career high average of 194. Her single game high score was 279.

- Louise Fulton was inducted into the Women's International Bowling Congress Hall of Fame in 2001.

MIKE AULBY

Career Facts:

- Mike won the PBA Rookie of the Year Award in 1979.

- He was named PBA Player of the Year in 1985 and 1995 and has 27 titles to his credit.

- Mike was the first bowler to win the Grand Slam. He also pioneered the Super Slam by winning a fifth major title, the 1998 Touring Players Championship.

- Mike was inducted into the PBA Hall of Fame in 1996.

CHECK IT OUT

Read more about rubberband duckpin bowling at
http://wikipedia.org
Type "duckpin bowling" in the Search field.

Superstars of the Game

Children having fun in bowling centers today will be the stars of the sport in the future.

WALTER RAY WILLIAMS JR.

Career Facts:

- Walter Ray has won 40 PBA tours.
- He won PBA Player of the Year Awards in 1986, 1993, 1996, 1997, 1998, and 2003.
- Walter Ray has won the Harry Smith Point Leader Award five times. He has won the George Young High Average Award four times.
- He was the first player to make more than $2 million in his bowling career.
- Walter Ray was inducted into the PBA Hall of Fame in 1995.

PETE WEBER

Career Facts:

- Pete is the son of well-known bowler Dick Weber. He joined his father in the PBA Hall of Fame in 1998.
- Pete was Rookie of the Year in 1980.
- He holds 31 PBA tour titles.
- He bowled a 299 score in the semifinal game at the Great Lakes Classic in 2001.

KELLY KULICK

Career Facts:

- Kelly won gold in the 1999 WTBA World Championships in the United Arab Emirates.
- She was All-American every year at Morehead State University. She played on three Team USA bowling squads.
- Kelly also played in the U.S. National Amateur Championships in 2000.
- She was chosen as Women's Pro Rookie of the Year by *Bowling Digest* in 2001.

PARKER BOHN III

Career Facts:

- Parker has 30 PBA titles. This makes him fifth on the all time list.
- Parker won the Sportsmanship Award in 1990, 1991, 1992, and 1993.
- He won PBA Player of the Year in 1999 and 2002.
- In 1999 and 2002, Parker was the Harry Smith Point Leader and received the George Young High Average Award.
- Parker was inducted into the PBA Hall of Fame in 2000.

Staying Healthy

Players need to be healthy to bowl their best. Fruits and vegetables provide most of the essential vitamins and minerals needed to stay healthy. Carbohydrates, such as bread, rice, and pasta, provide long-lasting energy. Protein builds muscles. Meat is a good source of protein. Dairy products, such as milk, yogurt, and cheese, provide calcium. Calcium keeps bones healthy and strong. A bowler should eat a balanced diet. This means eating foods from all the food groups.

Some people think that bowling is not a physical sport. This is not true. Players must be physically fit to bowl at a high level. They have to twist, stretch, and bend many times while bowling.

Eating colorful fruits and vegetables such as purple eggplant, white cauliflower, green grapes, yellow corn, and red apples keeps bowlers healthy.

Strong, flexible muscles are important for a bowler's game. Bowlers are more likely to make errors and to injure themselves when their muscles are tired and weak. Weight training once or twice a week helps maintain and build strong muscles.

Stretching before and after a game is important. Stretching helps keep players loose. Bowlers should warm up their arm muscles by doing arm circles. Running on the spot will warm up legs. Once muscles are warmed up, toe touches and lunges will stretch leg muscles. To stretch their arm muscles, players raise an arm over their head and bend it down to try to touch their shoulder blades. Then they stretch their other arm in the same way.

When exercising, bowlers should wear comfortable clothing that allows freedom of movement.

Lifting dumbbells can help strengthen arms. Bowlers need strong arms to lift heavy bowling balls.

Bowling Brain Teasers

Test your bowling knowledge by trying to answer these brain teasers!

Q In what year was 10-pin bowling invented?

A It was invented in 1870.

Q Who were the first bowlers?

A Sir Flanders Petrie believes that Ancient Egyptians may have been the first bowlers.

Q What does a player need to bowl?

A A player needs bowling shoes and a bowling ball.

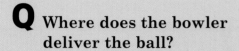

Q Where does the bowler deliver the ball?

A A player delivers the ball from the approach.

Q In the early years of bowling, how were pins set up?

A Pin boys set them up by hand.

Q What are the four types of bowling shots?

A The four types of bowling shots are the hook ball, curve ball, straight ball, and backup ball.

LEISURE · TIME

Glossary

amateur: a player who does not play for money

approach: the area before the foul line

automatic pinsetter: a machine that resets fallen pins

ball return: an underground tunnel through which the ball travels to return to the bowler

Egyptologist: a scientist who studies Ancient Egypt

governs: rules

gutter: a channel on either side of a bowling lane to catch balls that roll off the lane

hook: curve to the left

individual sport: a sport in which each person works toward his or her own best score

rosin: a sticky substance that is obtained from pine trees

rubberband duckpin: a form of bowling popular in parts of the United States during the 1930s. Pins are shorter and wider than pins today. Rubber bands circle each pin to increase their bounce.

Index

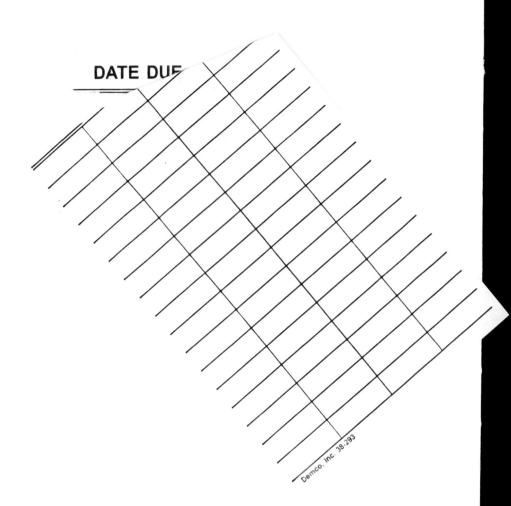

DATE DUE

Demco. Inc. 38-293